30 Ways to Sell Your Cakes

How to profit from your Cake Decorating Hobby or Business.

30 Ways to Sell Your Cakes

© 2018 Eme Bassey

All rights reserved. This book or any portion thereof
may not be reproduced or used in any manner whatsoever
without the express written permission of the publisher
except for the use of brief quotations in a book review.

DEDICATION
For Azuka.
… because there are always better days ahead.

I have a gift for you.

As a thank you for buying my book, I'd like to give you free access to my video training:

How to turn a Conversation into a Sale."

Go to www.cakeplc.com/30ways to watch the video.

START HERE
9
- 1. START WHERE YOU ARE
12
- 2. CHOOSE A NICHE
14
- 3. MAKE A SHOWCASE CAKE
17
- 4. RAISE YOUR PRICES
19
- 5. GET SOME TESTIMONIALS
21
- 6. MAKE A HIRE-ME PACK
23
- 7. GET FRIDGE MAGNETS
26
- GET OUT THERE
28
- 8. PICK UP THE PHONE
29
- 9. ASK FOR A REFERRAL
31

- 10. GET AN INTRODUCTION
35
- 11. GIVE THEM A TASTE
37
- 12. ALWAYS, ALWAYS BE INVITING
39
- TAKE IT OUT AND ABOUT
41
- 13. JOIN SOMETHING. JOIN EVERYTHING
42
- 14. TAKE A WALK OR A DRIVE
44
- 15. SELL AT MARKET STALLS
46
- 16. TEACH A CLASS
50
- 17. ATTEND EVENTS
52
- CONNECT AND COLLABORATE
54
- 18. YOUR EXISTING CUSTOMERS

55
- 19. EVENT PLANNERS AND VENUES
57
- 20. PEOPLE WHO MEET REGULARLY
59
- 21. COMPLIMENTARY BUSINESSES
61
- 22. INFLUENCERS
63
- 23. CHARITIES AND CAUSES
65
- WHAT ABOUT ONLINE TACTICS?
67
- 24. GOOGLE LOCAL
70
- 25. YOUTUBE
71
- 26. SOCIAL MEDIA
72
- 27. FACEBOOK ADVERTISING
73
- 28. JOIN A FACEBOOK GROUP

74
- 29. BUILD AN EMAIL LIST
77
- 30. REGISTER ON AN ONLINE DIRECTORY.
78
- WWW.CAKEPLC.COM
80
- ABOUT THE AUTHOR
81

START HERE…

You're here!
That automatically puts you in the top 10% of cake decorators who recognise the need to invest in themselves to grow their business.

Welcome! (Join me for a brief happy dance)

You know the value of what you do and are ready to share your cake talents with the world and get paid well for it too.

*That is why it's time to take control of your cake business and that starts with **being intentional about marketing and selling your cakes.***

If you don't do this, you will be at the mercy of bargain-hunting, nightmare customers.

However if you get into the habit of marketing and selling and make it a part of your everyday activities, you will build a cake business that you love and that supports you and your family for years to come.

I am going to tell you what I have said to the hundreds of cake decorators I have taught over the years.

Do not be afraid.

That's it.

It is much much easier than you think, so do not become overwhelmed. Start with 3 or 4 of the tips and take action and the results you get will encourage you to try other tips.

Keep this book handy and use it as a source of ideas to keep things fresh.

I know you can do this. You became a cake

decorator. You probably taught yourself a lot of what you know. This makes me know that you are creative, hard working, compassionate and fearless.

You have what it takes. Now go and use those same qualities to bring in customers that love you and want to do business with you.

Eme Bassey
www.cakeplc.com

1. START WHERE YOU ARE

MAKE A LIST OF EVERYONE YOU KNOW

I mean *everyone.*

This is your first list.

These are the people that you are going to start with.

You are going to start talking to them so that you get into the habit of reaching out and connecting to people. You will practice introducing yourself, and asking for what you want. You will practice building rapport, starting relationships and strengthening connections.

Your first list will also hold valuable connections to future customers so everyone on your list is important - even if they hate cake!

Your First list will be

Friends, relatives, acquaintances, neighbours, kids

Your first list will include your existing customers. Anyone who would recognise you on the street or recognise your number on the phone goes on the list. This will include your Facebook friends and fans, your email list if you have one, your coworkers, the mums in your school and so on.

Everyone is important. This list will be anything from 100 to 250 people.

Now, understand that the people on your first list DO NOT all have to become your customers.

Yes they could be potential customers but they could also be your supporters, friends, referrers, introducers, taste-testers, idea-givers big-fish connectors and so on.

You will be surprised that this list could yield you more customers than you imagine possible.

2. CHOOSE A NICHE

WHAT DO YOU WANT TO BE KNOWN FOR?

CLAIM A NICHE OR SPECIALTY THAT YOU ARE GOING TO IDENTIFY YOURSELF WITH.

This may sound counter-intuitive but narrowing down to a specific niche will benefit you better than being known generally for "making cakes".

Your niche could be a geographical area that you serve or a particular kind of person or industry you serve (lawyers? Estate agents? Yummy mummies?).

Your niche could also be the kind of cakes you want to be known for. This could be wedding cakes or kids birthday cakes or office party cakes or cupcakes or baby shower cakes or crazy standing sculpted cakes. Focus on your strengths as well as what you think would be the money makers in your town.

You can narrow down your niche as much as you want. Do you want to be known for elegant wedding cakes? sugar flowers? Chocolate wedding cakes? Baby shower cakes? Hen party cakes? Engagement cakes? ...the list is endless.

This will NOT necessarily be the ONLY kinds of cakes you make but this is what you want to be KNOWN for.

The reason why I STRONGLY suggest you pick a niche is that it makes your marketing that much easier because:

- It will help you target your customers more precisely
- It is easier to introduce yourself.
- It builds your credibility when you are a master of one instead of a jack of all cake trades.
- it is also easier for your customer to find you or better still DECIDE to work with you because they know that you are expert at the EXACT thing they want.
- Your customer self-selects.
- Its easier to get word of mouth referrals because the person automatically knows WHO to introduce you to.

If you are not comfortable with this idea, you can call it your SPECIALTY.

What's your specialty? What is your niche? Claim it now.

3. MAKE A SHOWCASE CAKE

SHOW OFF YOUR BEST WORK

Don't wait for a customer to make an order.

You can be the customer.

Make a cake or a set of cakes showcasing your best skills and your unique style.

Make it as eye-catching, striking and beautiful as you can.

Photograph it nicely and then put it up everywhere. On your website, Facebook, brochure, flyers. instagram etc.

Get into the habit of always showing your best work. Not every single cake you make should go on your fb page or website.

Be intentional about choosing the ones that

show your skills in the best light.

4. RAISE YOUR PRICES

WHAT? THE PRICING THING AGAIN?

Lets look at the price thing again shall we?

I am 98% convinced that your price is STILL too low. So here's what I am going to ask you to do right now.

Raise your prices by (at least) 10% or £10 or $10. Just that little raise will add more than 10% to your bottom line. (Up to 30% in fact! - for the same amount of work!)

Announcing a price increase might be a way to get an influx of customers.

For instance, you could announce that your prices are going up in 28 days or "from the 1st day of next month" and that you can confirm orders at the old price for up to 6 months in advance. That may very well make people commit to ordering their wedding/christmas/birthday cakes and putting down a deposit for their order.

Therefore you have an influx of customers who want to get their orders in **before** the price goes up. This tactic could even get you customers who want to book you months in advance just so they get the old prices.

The second reason your should increase your prices is that you will **attract a better quality of customer** and push away the bargain hunters. Furthermore, as you get better at marketing, you will learn how to attract the exact kind of customers you want to work with.

5. GET SOME TESTIMONIALS

RECOMMENDATIONS FROM HAPPY CUSTOMERS ARE PURE GOLD!

Testimonials are a powerful way to get customers. It is a great form of "word of mouth" marketing.

Think of all the times you look at reviews and testimonials on items in a shop before making a decision to buy. It is the same with your customers and could *make the difference between an undecided customer and a commitment to purchase.*

People may or may not believe what you say but they are much more likely to believe what other people say about you. Another thing testimonials does is that it helps the person put themselves in the shoes of the customer. When a testimonial says "I used to be like this" or "I was looking for this" and this product helped me get this or do this, the person hearing it gets a chance to say "me too..."

Find three or five or ten of your best customers and ask them to send you a testimonial.

Sometimes you have letters nor cards that people had written to you or comments that people had left on your website or Facebook page. When this happens, go ahead and ask for permission to share this.

Don't wait for these occasional testimonials or reviews. Go out and actively ask for them. Make a few calls, send an email or talk to someone on Facebook. You could even go a step further and shoot a video testimonial at the event that you made a cake for.

Now put those testimonials everywhere. Use them on your fb posts, pages, website, brochures, YouTube channel and even in conversations with other customers.

6. MAKE A HIRE-ME PACK

MAKE IT EASY FOR PEOPLE TO WORK WITH YOU

This is different from a brochure or flyer. It is what you would give to interested prospects to help them get to know you better and make their order quicker when they are ready to do so.

You can make your hire me pack as DIY or as professional as you can afford. Depending on your style, budget and target market this could be a whimsical scrapbook or an elegant luxury photobook.

A basic hire me pack could be printed on Blurb.com, created with Canva.com or printed at the library, local printshop or done scrapbook style. You could even hire a graphic designer to layout something really professional/quirky/whimsical for you that shows off your style.

Your hire me pack should contain:

- Your best cake photographs (two or three) showcasing your style and your specialty
- Your contact details
- A complimentary card or fridge magnet with contact number.
- Your story
- Your flavours
- Social Proof: Testimonials, names of previous customers if applicable (This works well if you make cakes for organisations or celebrities)
- How to order.
- How to book a consultation
- Questionnaire about their events, personal preferences, etc
- Enquiry form or pre-stamped postcard to send to you when they are ready to order.
- How to book a tasting consultation session (paid)
- A cover letter if applicable.
- discount vouchers, referral information etc etc

The hire me pack should either go before you or better still be sent after you have made initial contact with your prospective customer.

It could also be a good talking point when you have a consultation.

Now, you don't need to have a hire me pack. But when you do, you immediately raise your profile with the customer. It shows you know what you are doing.

Most importantly, It makes it easer for your customer to find you, make their order, answers their questions and shows them how to work with you. People are busy and they have more choices. The easier you make it for them to work with you the better your chance of securing cake orders. .

7. GET FRIDGE MAGNETS

A WAY TO STAND OUT AND STAY VISIBLE

This is even better than business cards. IMHO.

For one thing it makes you stand out and makes you memorable because it's unusual.

Especially when you have built up rapport.

Be very intentional about who you give these to. You want to have built such a good rapport with the person that you can "insist" they stick it on their fridge and give you a call when they need their next cake.

Make the message compelling, and eye catching or even funny. Keep it brief and add a bold contact number. I have a magnet for the handyman on my fridge. Its easily accessible and I don't have to go searching for the contact when I need his services.

Definitely give magnets to your current customers. In fact, if your old customers have not heard from you in a while, this is a great way to reconnect. You can call them on the phone and tell them you are sending them a gift to show your appreciation. Do it for your best customers.

You could also include a magnet in the thank you card you send after their cake order asking them to stick it up and give you a call anytime they think of cake.

This is a great excuse to follow up on a potential customer as well as strengthen the bond with a current customer. And it keeps you front of mind and easily accessible if they need a cake or better still if they have a friend that needs a cake.

Check out www.vistaprint.com for sweet deals on inexpensive fridge magnets. Alternatively search for custom magnets online if you want your magnets to have specific shapes.

GET OUT THERE

Phew! You are now set up and ready to get out there and get customers.

You now have your list of "prospects".

You have your hire me pack ready. Your showcase cakes are being shown everywhere (as best you can).

Now it's time to start reaching out to people on your list.

Your relationships are a big part of the success of your business so this is not the time to be shy.

Take baby steps. Everyday. That's all you need for now. Do something everyday to grow your cake business.

Let's continue…

8. PICK UP THE PHONE

DO THIS EVERYDAY!

So here is the thing…
You may need a special kind of phone.
You have to make sure it is the kind of phone that doesn't bite!
Okay so I'm just messing with you. Just to let you know that it doesn't have to be complicated.

Just pick up the phone and call people.

Smile and dial. Smile and dial!!!
Start with your list. (From Tip #1)

Before every call, decide what the purpose of the call is. Decide what you want as the outcome.

Examples: You may be calling to
- Announce something (a special offer, a new shop opening, your new pop-up stall
 - Invite them to something - Visit your market

stall, attend a tasting event, attend a holiday class
- Ask for a Referrals (from existing/recent customers)
- Ask for an introduction.
- Ask for Ideas, advice, help. People love to help.
- Ask to send them free samples in exchange for feedback/testimonials
- Ask to send them free samples "just because"
- Catch up and rebuild a stale relationship (and don't forget to tell them what you are up to these days.
- Just to say hello and find out how they are doing
- Don't just hang up the phone! Schedule the next call or meeting or coffee or lunch. Keep in touch and keep the conversation going.

Everyday in every way you must be marketing. ***Every call may not end in a sale but every call should have a purpose.***

9. ASK FOR A REFERRAL

GET YOUR CUSTOMERS TO GET YOU MORE CUSTOMERS.

It is possible to build your entire business on referrals.

No fancy websites, no millions of Facebook fans, just word of mouth. There is a method to this.

Don't expect people to naturally tell their friends about you even if they love your cakes. You have to ask them to recommend you to their friends.

First of all (obviously) you have to deliver a great cake and great customer care.

The best time to ask for a referral is when you are taking the cake order or after delivering the order.

In the process of taking the cake order, you would say this:

"I get most of my customers by word of mouth so if you love the cake you are going to get, would you be happy to recommend me to one or two of your friends?"

Make sure you make this verbal agreement. Most people would say yes.

When you deliver the cake, remind them that they promised to recommend you to friends and either ask them to call the friends and give you the friend's address to send them a hire me pack and schedule a no-obligation call or visit.

Pro tip:
Be specific about the "person" you would like your customer or friend to recommend you to. That makes it easier for them to come up with names.

For example you would say:
"Do you know of any mums with young children?" or

"Do you know of any ladies getting married this year? or
"Do you know any office managers" or
seniors graduating this year...
"Someone expecting a baby..."

You get the idea?

Always **be as specific as possible when asking for a referral.**

For example, say "Do you know someone that would like a cake for her child's birthday/bridal shower/office party/graduation party....

Then ask for their number or ask them to call/email them and tell them you will be calling/emailing/sending brochure/card/website/fb page/hire-me pack.

You could also offer them a freebie (cupcakes?) or a discount for every customer they send your way. So you continue by saying "As a thank you I always give a box of cupcakes or ££$$ off your next cake order or a free cake after X number of customers.

Apart from asking for a referral when you are

taking cake orders, you can also call up old customers as well as people in your contact list to ask for referrals.

10. GET AN INTRODUCTION

WHEN YOU ARE TARGETING A BIG FISH CLIENT

This is similar to getting referrals but works especially well when you are trying to land a particular "big fish" client.

Even though it is possible for you to turn up at someone's doorstep, getting an introduction is always better than cold calling someone who doesn't know you from a can of paint.

An introductions adds credibility and increases the likelihood that the person you are meeting will trust you - because he trusts the person that is introducing you.

In fact, and this is important, **your first list (tip #1) is sometimes not as important as the people they will introduce you to.**

This is because your first list will probably be very close friends. They have seen you in your pyjamas, they knew you as an unserious college student. They may have known you when you were a naked baby and seen you at your worst. So your first list may not even take you as seriously as someone that they introduce you to.

While it is helpful to get an introduction, do not be discouraged if you don't know anyone that knows that particular person you would like to work with.

There are other ways that with a bit of courage and strategy you can still get in front of your dream clients without an introduction.

11. GIVE THEM A TASTE

GIVE THEM A TASTE OF YOUR DELICIOUS CAKES.

You can do this in two ways:
1. Send out samples or
2. Host a tasting event

Sample boxes: .
Weekly, monthly or fortnightly.
Four to six of your best flavours. Cut in chinks or slices or as cupcakes. Packaged prettily for delivery. These samples could be free or you could charge a flat fee for this box of cake slices..

Offer this to people as a first taste of what you can offer. This is a great way to have a second contact or a follow up to an initial phone call and could lead to a sales conversation.

This works for any kind of cake customer and is a great conversation starter. Whether its the mum for her future kids parties or the office for their upcoming office party, a sample pack will move the sales process along.

If you are wondering what to do when you have your first list, this is a great ice breaker. If they seem to be interested in your services, you can ask to send them a sample taster box and follow up for when they are ready to order.

Tasting events:
These do not have to be complicated. You can arrange this with a venue or in your shop, a client's home or a community venue. I have often set up free cakes at the coffee morning organised by a local church and just asked for donations to be made to the church. I would set up four flavours of cakes and serve them up in slices. I have got cake orders from the people who attended and there is also goodwill created in the community..

Remember that marketing is not simply selling cakes but also creating visibility and building reputation and goodwill.

12. ALWAYS, ALWAYS BE INVITING

YES I SAID IT TWICE

The lesson is to ALWAYS be inviting people to something. Whether you are talking in person, over the phone or online.

As time goes on you will think of more ways but I will give you a few suggestions here.

- Invite your friend to coffee and ask for their advice.

Other invitations could be:

A special offer of the month.

A flavour taste testing event

To receive your weekly sample boxes

To attend a class you are teaching with their

kids

To host a tasting event for their friends (You will bring the cake!)

To see you at your next market stall day.

Even if you don't have anything to invite people to, invite them to the next phone call or conversation.

These are just a few but I am sure you can come up with more depending on where you live and who you are in contact with.

Always be inviting...

TAKE IT OUT AND ABOUT

Some people will love the following suggestions and some would hate the idea of putting themselves "out there".

Keep an open mind as you read on. You will see how easy and fun it can be.

It's all about building relationships and making yourself known and that is a good thing.

Think long-term with these tactics but trust me they are worth the investment of time and effort.

13. JOIN SOMETHING. JOIN EVERYTHING

ENRICH YOUR LIFE

Most of what has been said here focuses on local marketing opportunities and strategies.

Joining a group, club or organisation is a great way to get involved in the community, make connections, build relationships and from there get cake orders, referrals introductions and other forms of support and help in your cake business.

It could be the PTA, local church, synagogue or mosque, A country club, golf club, book club, knitting circle, walking club, mums group, chamber of commerce, rotary club, community action group, free groups, residents association, paid groups, masterminds, and on and on.

When you are in the group, have fun. It's not

all about your cakes. Be a friend. Not to sell your cakes but genuinely be a friend.They may not buy your cakes but they may tell their friends about you.

Be helpful: Answer questions. Solve problems. Be a listener. Be generous. Share information. Share access. Connect people to one another. Always find a way to make person's day better because this keeps you top of mind.

Being part of a group is great for you and for your business. No matter how high tech we get these days nothing can compare to the bonds that can be created by in-person face to face connections and conversations. IT enriches your life in every way and not just your business.

14. TAKE A WALK OR A DRIVE

GET INSPIRATION RIGHT AT YOUR DOORSTEP

Walk or drive around your neighbourhood and look at all the businesses, shops, churches, community centres, offices, and institutions.

Now, brainstorm different ways you can work with each of them. Write down your ideas and then take action on each one to reach out.

Make a call, send a letter, send a sample, propose an event that you can co-host, donate a prize for a competition, suggest a regular supply service.

The list is endless. Think outside the box. You will be surprised at what you come up with if you just open your eyes to the possibilities around you.

Just today I took my son to a soft play area and

discovered that they hire out their venue for kids parties. They have a little cafe with drinks and food but you guessed it NO CAKE.

This kind of place would be happy to hear from you with your selection of kids cakes that they can add to their "package".

15. SELL AT MARKET STALLS

GET INTO THE COMMUNITY AND GET FEEDBACK

This is a great way to get yourself out into the community and to find out what your clients need and how to better serve them.

It doesn't have to be every week or every month but it is a good idea to plan one or more "outings" for your cake business each year.

When you are baking for friends and family they may tell you that your chocolate cake is the best they have ever tasted. Their opinions don't count because they may be just being nice. Or not.

Getting feedback from strangers about the taste and the looks of your cakes is invaluable. Getting to know who they are and what is important to your potential customers is invaluable.

Never make assumptions that you know what people want. Your community may want plain and simple while you may be thinking gourmet and haute cuisine - or the other way round.

You may find that the cakes that you think are "no big deal" are the ones that people rush for.
Market stalls give you great feedback that way.

This could be as simple as the fun day or summer fair in your kids schools or taking part in trade shows, wedding fairs, farmers markets, holiday markets, bake sales and so on.

Find out their rules.
Check the fees.
Make a budget
Make a menu
Make your signage and price list.
Make tasters.

Make it pretty and inviting (check pinterest.com for inspiration.

Be friendly and interested in people.

Remember also to put the details on your

Facebook page or website to invite your fans to come see and taste in person and of course meet you.

Market stalls will also help you get practice in building rapport with people and getting to the heart of their needs.

Note that you can also set up a stall if you want to demonstrate cake decorating and advertise your classes.

Do a quick google search and find stalls and events close to you that you can take part in.

UK http://www.stallfinder.com/
Australia http://www.localmarketguide.com.au/
USA http://search.ams.usda.gov/farmersmarkets/
Canada http://www.farmersmarketonline.ca/markets

Please note that it takes a while to find your groove and turn a profit in farmers markets. If you find you love it them invest some time in improving and growing that venture.

However for the purpose of what I am saying here, your primary focus is in getting your name out there, getting to know your customers and building relationships. These could and should lead to future cake orders but ***do not go to the market trying to make money or you will be disappointed***.

Instead see it as an investment and a marketing activity and look to at least break even.

16. TEACH A CLASS

INCREASE YOUR EXPERT STATUS

This is the similar to the farmers markets strategy.

The aim is to create goodwill in your community and get to know your customers.

The added bonus is that if you run classes it can

- Supplement your income during slow periods
- Position you as an expert

You don't have to teach complicated classes. Keep it simple. For fun and leisure.

Examples are Cupcake making and cupcake decorating classes, Others could be introduction to cake decorating, figure modelling, baking, gingerbread house making and similar half-day classes.

Offer this to your customers and their friends and/or their kids.

You could do it in a dedicated venue or in your customers home.
Again it could be seasonal or once a month.

We are talking about teaching as *part of your marketing strategy.*

However if you find you love teaching and have a natural gift for it then by all means go further and deeper and bigger and really teach!

17. ATTEND EVENTS

GET OUT THERE AND MEET PEOPLE

Attend an event.

These should NOT necessarily be cake related.

Ideally if you have identified your niche or specialty then you want to go to places where you will find people that would be attracted to and need the kind of cakes you make. If you make cakes for kids, then go to places that mums go!

Formal networking events are NOT your first choice either. This may be an option if you can pull it off without seeming desperate or grabby.

Instead look for other formal and informal events such as

- local classes - free and paid. Online and offline

- Seminars. Workshops, Conferences and Conventions
- Shows, Festivals, Fairs, Fetes
- Weddings, parties and other swanky gatherings.

You want places you can go to get inspiration and get a feel of how your potential customer lives works and plays.

You also want to attend events where you will have a chance to speak to and interact with people.

Always be on the lookout for ways that you can help. Always be thinking of how to make their day better or their life better.

Talk to people. Introduce yourself and what you do when appropriate.

But you are not going there to peddle your wares. You are going to meet people and talk to them and get ideas and find opportunities.

Be open to opportunities and most importantly have fun!

CONNECT AND COLLABORATE

Now its time to run with the big dogs.

Okay, maybe medium-sized dogs.

Okay maybe not dogs, maybe you are a lion or giraffe girl or guy...

I digress... (just making sure I still have your attention)

The point is that now you are being strategic.

Remember that even though you start where you are, you don't have to stay where you are.

Take action... Take one action - big or small - every single day to move towards your goal.

You've got this.

18. YOUR EXISTING CUSTOMERS

AN EASY SOURCE OF SALES

It has been said that it is up to 10 times easier/cheaper to get an old customer to buy from you than it is to get a new customer. So it makes sense to start here when you want to get your next cake orders.

Call your three best customers or your three most recent customers.

Catch up with them (how are you? and family and work? etc.)

Tell them you really enjoyed working with them and would love to make their next cake.

Then ask them when their next celebration is. If they tell you about a birthday or baby shower, spend time asking about their plans and "imagining" with them how the par ty/dinner/

barbecue could be.

Ask them whether you could put them in your calendar and schedule a call to design/plan their next cake.

You may or may not sell on the spot but now they are ready for when you call for the consultation or to take their order.

You don't have to follow these exact steps but use your initiative and always try and get a date commitment.

19. EVENT PLANNERS AND VENUES

ASSOCIATIONS AND COLLABORATIONS - PART 1.

Event planners and venues are a great group of people to work for.

It is actually possible to build your entire business with these as your main customers.

To be honest it takes a bit of work, strategy, determination and planning to be successful at this.

However, if you have built a good brand and reputation then this is worth going after as a marketing strategy.

Wedding planners, party planners and event venues are a different market from your average end-user so again you would need a bit of tweaking to your approach to getting a chance to work with them successfully.

It's different but certainly do-able. The key is to be professional in your presentation and service.

20. PEOPLE WHO MEET REGULARLY

ASSOCIATIONS AND COLLABORATIONS - PART 2.

This is where you should do some detective work because it differs from place to place.

People who meet regularly could be a good source of regular income.

Think of people who meet regularly in your area and how you can supply them with regular cakes or cupcakes.

- Chamber of commerce
- Community groups.
- Office meetings
- Mums and toddler groups
- Business networking groups
- Breakfast business meetings
- The PTA of your kid's school
- Church, mosques, synagogue...

- Meetups! If you find a list of meet-ups in your area you will find one or two that meet for coffee and - you guessed it- cake! And even if they don't you can always contact the organiser and offer to supply cakes to their next venue.

Bigger one-off events like seminars, conferences, retreats and workshops, food shows and even festivals are another source of business.

Your job is to find the groups and gatherings close to you, research their needs and requirements and then communicate with them and offer your services.

21. COMPLIMENTARY BUSINESSES

ASSOCIATIONS AND COLLABORATIONS 3.

You are looking for people who are in contact with and serve your potential customers.

Your aim is to develop working partnerships with them where you trade services or collaborate on marketing campaigns.

Here are just a few examples:
Your local florist,
hairdressers, nail salons,
restaurants and cafes
wedding venues
Wedding professionals: planners, photographers, caterers, decorators,
stationers, dress designers and so on.

Show them your work (brochure, website, pictures etc)
and/or better still take in taster samples.

The easiest way to start is to exchange your services, seeing as you sell to the same kind of customers. E.g. 10% discount voucher for them to give to their customers and they would do the same for you.

For caterers and party planners you can give them special rates to give to their customers or they can order direct from you at a good price and put a mark-up on your cakes to sell on to their customers.

There are no hard and fast rules here.

The more you are able to build good rapport and strong relationships with these people the easier it will be to come up with different ways to work together; organise campaigns, special offers and host events together.

22. INFLUENCERS

ASSOCIATIONS AND COLLABORATIONS 4.

Once in a while you are fortunate to come in contact with a person that has a lot of contacts and connections. This can be both online and in your circle of influence.

This could be anyone from the "queen bee" of the mummy mafia to your chatty neighbour or your pastor's wife. This can also be people with large online followings on social media.

Do not discount people because they don't appear to be "connected" - you might find that being nice to that receptionist or "gate-keeper" is what will get you inside information on how to meet the big boss man!

I don't advocate seeking people out unless you have something in common with them, something to offer and some level of relationship or rapport with them.

Secondly, you should find a way to add value to their lives and be a giver and helper before asking for help.

Be confident and hold your own. And when it is appropriate and you want to ask for help, always be specific about who you would like them to introduce you to or tell you about. Be specific.

The great thing about such people is that most of them are usually helpful and generous.

When it comes to influencers, the quality of your relationship is the most important thing and what you invest into them will determine how much you get out of it.

Give first before asking.

23. CHARITIES AND CAUSES

A SMARTER WAY TO GIVE "FREE" CAKES

As cake decorators we are often invited to "donate" a cake to a charity or a cause. this does not always result in future orders. (in fact most times it doesn't)

If done right, you can get a lot of business and new customers this way. It all depends on your strategy. Here is a smart strategy:

If a club or charity wants to raise money with your help, instead of just baking and sending them a cake, you can create a special offer just for ALL THEIR MEMBERS or INVITEES for a SPECIFIC period of time during their fundraising.

Then you ask the charity to give out the offer (e.g. gift certificates or discount vouchers) to their list of guests or members. One voucher per person

On the voucher you state clearly that part of the profits from the cake order goes to support the charity. You and the charity both publicise the event. They are therefore more committed to your getting more orders because the more you sell the more money they get.

The result is win-win. More new customers, more sales and you supported a good cause which is good for your reputation..

This is a better strategy. Tweak as needed. The important thing is to get the most out of this association and get direct access to the clients and friends of the charity

You don't have to wait to be approached by a charity. You can find a good charity and propose this kind of arrangement to them.

WHAT ABOUT ONLINE TACTICS?

FOCUS ON LOCAL NOT GLOBAL.

Here's the thing.

There are many reasons why your marketing as a cake decorator should focus on local. It makes sense to find customers that live and work near where your cakes are made.

This is why most of the tactics I am giving are focused on local marketing strategies. However, there are a number of things you can do online to support your efforts.

Whatever online tactics you use, always think local. Use geotags on instagram. Join local Facebook groups. Target locally with Facebook and google ads.

Don't get caught up in the hype of numbers of followers on social media.

Think local.

In my experience, there are many things you could do online that can be a waste of your time when it comes to getting customers through your doors and money into your bank account.

So, you must weigh everything you want to do online and don't get caught up with chasing after tricks and tactics or doing what you see someone else doing.

Think it though.

Ask yourself - Would it be better to spend my money on Facebook adverts rather than a fancy website? What is the purpose of my website? Can I justify it? There is no right or wrong answer. The answer is what is the next best thing to do right now for your business to help you achieve your goals. That is what is important.

I am not knocking websites. In fact I build websites all the time for my clients. All I am saying is that there must be a purpose and strategy as well as a measurable result for whatever efforts you make online.

I am also saying that you do not need to have a website to have a thriving respectable business in your community.

There are many opportunities for a cake decorator in the online marketing space and that is a conversation for another book. However in this handbook, I have stripped it down to the essentials to avoid wasting time and money.

These are the online tactics I recommend if you are a cake decorator wishing to sell cakes to their local community.

24. GOOGLE LOCAL

REGISTER ON GOOGLE LOCAL

Its a long-ish process but worth the effort.

Register on this and on as many local directories as possible. (Yelp, local london, etc)

www.google.co.uk/business

25. YOUTUBE

MAKE A YOUTUBE VIDEO

Use the keywords "best cupcakes / cakes/ wedding cakes in___ add the name of your city or town. This video has a good chance of appearing high on google search when people search for cakes in your area.

26. SOCIAL MEDIA

MASTER ONE SOCIAL MEDIA CHANNEL

Don't try to be in all of them. Great choices for cake decorators are Facebook, instagram and youtube because of they are great for visual content and have the potential to reach many people.

Pinterest is great as well but only worth it if you have a website or blog.

27. FACEBOOK ADVERTISING

CONSIDER FACEBOOK ADVERTISING

There is not enough space here to talk about this but fb ads are a great opportunity because you can target locally - that is find people who live a few miles from you.

A few quick tips:
1. Use video ads.
2. have a one-time awesome offer.
3. Collect emails and phone numbers so you can follow up.
4. Use the Facebook pixel
5. Use look-alike audiences

28. JOIN A FACEBOOK GROUP

But first, allow me A LITTLE RANT (PLEASE)

One thing that makes me crazy is when I see cake decorators spend all their time on Facebook groups dedicated to CAKE PEOPLE!

For crying out loud!

If you are looking for customers on Facebook, why spend all your time online hanging around cake people. I love cake people and that is why I spend a lot of time creating training for you but I will tell you this: STOP HANGING AROUND CAKE DECORATORS ON FACEBOOK GROUPS!!!

Go hang around your potential customers. Make those endless hours on Facebook count for something.

Look for groups online where brides hang out

if you are a wedding cake maker.

Hang around mums groups if you make cakes for kids.

And don't forget to look for groups that serve your local area - your city or state.

Join groups of coaches, photographers, event planners, gift directories, interior decorators, bloggers, caterers, restaurateurs, entrepreneurs. Womens groups of all kinds... The possibilities are endless.

Interact with the people on the group. Talk to people. Respond to comments. Answer questions. Be helpful. Don't be spammy but once to twice a month post a picture of your cakes there. I got this tip from a cake friend who joined a group for wedding gowns!

So now you see why it drives me crazy when I see cake decorators gathering in cake groups to whine and complain or bash and trash customers or seek for compliments and praise or worse still compare their cakes to others and make themselves feel bad. How is any of that going to add customers to your list or put money in your pocket?

Yes of course there are benefits of hanging around cake decorators. Your colleagues will give you feedback and support and share tips with you. But if you are looking for customers then you won't find them among your colleagues! Cake friends are not going to buy your cakes after all. (Rant over)

29. BUILD AN EMAIL LIST

YOUR MOST PROFITABLE ONLINE ACTIVITY

If you do only ONE thing online, build an email list.

End of.

Finito.

Nuff said.

Let me put it this way.

You will get more sales per person from your email list than any social media.

Build an email list. Then email them regularly.

- Make offers
- Tell stories, build relationship
- Update them on news

30. REGISTER ON AN ONLINE DIRECTORY.

JOIN "WE ARE CAKE MAKERS"

We Are Cake Makers is an online marketplace created to:

CONNECT CAKE MAKERS TO LOCAL CUSTOMERS.

Instagram @wearecakemakers

The marketplace is built and optimised specifically to help your local customers find you and order cakes from you online.

www.wearecakemakers.com

It's like ebay but for cake decorators

Members also enjoy a supportive community, decorating tutorials and masterclasses with the best up-to-date marketing tips tricks and techniques.

WWW.CAKEPLC.COM

Get more marketing tips at www.cakeplc.com

Cake PLC is a blog with Business, Marketing and Selling tips specifically for cake decorators. We curate and present the best marketing advice and support to help Cake decorators profit from their gifts and talents.

We also have a fun Facebook group. (Search for Cake PLC - Profit Learn Connect)

ABOUT THE AUTHOR

Eme Bassey is a Cake Decorating tutor, Author, blogger and
   Digital Marketing Strategist
   She calls herself a finder, big-dreamer, lover of all things handmade and a God-chaser.

Connect with me on
www.cakeplc.com